MW01407532

SQL QUICKSTART GUIDE

The Simplified Beginner's Guide To SQL

ClydeBank TECHNOLOGY

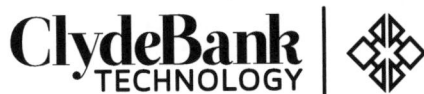

Copyright 2015 by ClydeBank Media - All Rights Reserved.

This document is geared towards providing exact and reliable information in regards to the topic and issue covered. The publication is sold with the idea that the publisher is not required to render accounting, officially permitted, or otherwise, qualified services. If advice is necessary, legal or professional, a practiced individual in the profession should be ordered.

From a Declaration of Principles which was accepted and approved equally by a Committee of the American Bar Association and a Committee of Publishers and Associations. In no way is it legal to reproduce, duplicate, or transmit any part of this document in either electronic means or in printed format. Recording of this publication is strictly prohibited and any storage of this document is not allowed unless with written permission from the publisher.

The information provided herein is stated to be truthful and consistent, in that any liability, in terms of inattention or otherwise, by any usage or abuse of any policies, processes, or directions contained within is the solitary and utter responsibility of the recipient reader. Under no circumstances will any legal responsibility or blame be held against the publisher for any reparation, damages, or monetary loss due to the information herein, either directly or indirectly. Respective authors own all copyrights not held by the publisher. The information herein is offered for informational purposes solely, and is universal as so. The presentation of the information is without contract or any type of guarantee assurance.

Trademarks: All trademarks are the property of their respective owners. The trademarks that are used are without any consent, and the publication of the trademark is without permission or backing by the trademark owner. All trademarks and brands within this book are for clarifying purposes only and are owned by the owners themselves, not affiliated with this document.

ClydeBank Media LLC is not associated with any organization, product or service discussed in this book. The publisher has made every effort to ensure that the information presented in this book was accurate at time of publication. All precautions have been taken in the preparation of this book. The publisher, author, editor and designer assume no responsibility for any loss, damage, or disruption caused by errors or omissions from this book, whether such errors or omissions result from negligence, accident, or any other cause.

Cover Illustration and Design: Katie Poorman, Copyright © 2015 by ClydeBank Media LLC
Interior Design: Katie Poorman, Copyright © 2015 by ClydeBank Media LLC

ClydeBank Media LLC
P.O Box 6561
Albany, NY 12206

Printed in the United States of America

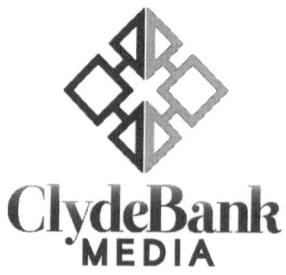

Copyright © 2015
ClydeBank Media LLC
www.clydebankmedia.com
All Rights Reserved

ISBN-13 : 978-1508767480

TABLE OF CONTENTS

Overview 6
    Sample Database 7
Introduction 8
    What Is SQL? 8
    Syntax and Structure 11
Chapter 1 : Retrieving Data With SQL 13
    The SELECT Statement 13
    The FROM Clause 15
    Limiting Data by Specifying Columns 15
    SQL Predicates 16
    Returning DISTINCT Rows 16
    TOP 17
    The WHERE Clause 19
    Comparison Operators 20
    Logical Operators 22
    Dealing With Ranges and Wildcards 24
    Operator Precedence 26
    The ORDER BY Clause 27
    Using Aliases with the AS Clause 29
    Selecting Records from Multiple Tables 30
    Including Excluded Data with OUTER JOIN 34
    NULL Values 37
Chapter 2 : Built-In Functions and Arithmetic Calculations 39
    COUNT 39
    SUM 41
    Other Functions 41
    Grouping Data with the GROUP BY Clause 43
    Limiting Group Results with HAVING 46

Chapter 3 : Entering and Modifying Data	47
INSERT Information INTO the Database	47
Updating Data	49
Deleting Data from Tables	50
Chapter 4 : Defining Databases	51
Creating/Deleting a Database	51
Data Types	52
Characters	53
Numerical Data	54
Date and Time	54
Defining Tables	55
Conclusion	58
Glossary	59
About ClydeBank Technology	60
More Books by ClydeBank Technology	61

OVERVIEW

A *database* is a collection of data consisting of a physical file residing on a computer. The collection of data in that file is stored in different *tables* where each row in the table is considered as a record. Every record is broken down into fields that represent single items of data describing a specific thing. For example, you can store information about a collection of book data inside a database. Information pertaining to the books themselves can be stored in a table called Books. Each book record can be stored in one table row with each specific piece of data such as book title, author, or price, stored into a separate field.

DATABASE → **TABLES** → **RECORDS**

More technically, a database can also be defined as an organized structured object stored on a computer consisting of data and metadata. Data, as previously explained, is the actual information stored in the database, while metadata is data about the data. *Metadata* describes the structure of the data itself, such as field length or datatype. For example, in a company database the value 6.95 stored in a field is data about the price of a specific product. The information that this is a number data stored to two decimal places and valued in dollars is metadata.

Databases are usually associated with software that allows for the data to be updated and queried. The software that manages the database is called a Relational Database Management System (***RDBMS***). These systems make storing data and returning results easier and more efficient by allowing different questions and commands to be posed to the database. Popular RDBMS software includes Oracle Database, Microsoft SQL Server, MySQL, and IBM DB2. Commonly, the RDBMS software itself is referred to as a database, although theoretically this would be a slight misnomer. When working with databases we will participate in the design, maintenance and administration of the database that supplies data to our website or application. In order to do this, however, we will need to access that data and also automate the process to allow other users to retrieve and perhaps even modify data without technical knowledge. To achieve this we will need to communicate with the database in a language it can interpret. Structured Query Language (*SQL*) will allow us to directly communicate with databases and is thus the subject of this book. In this book we will learn the basics of SQL. SQL is composed of commands that enable users to create database and table structures, perform various types of data manipulation and data administration and query the database in order to extract useful information.

Sample Database

The examples in this book use the Northwind Traders Access database, which is a sample database that comes with the Microsoft Office suite. The Northwind database contains sales data for a fictitious company called Northwind Traders, which imports and exports specialty foods from around the world. Depending on your Office version, the Northwind database might look slightly different, as it has evolved over time. Nevertheless, the examples use only those tables that have remained unchanged in each iteration.

Additionally, you can download the Northwind database from the following link:

http://www.geeksengine.com/article/download/Northwind.zip

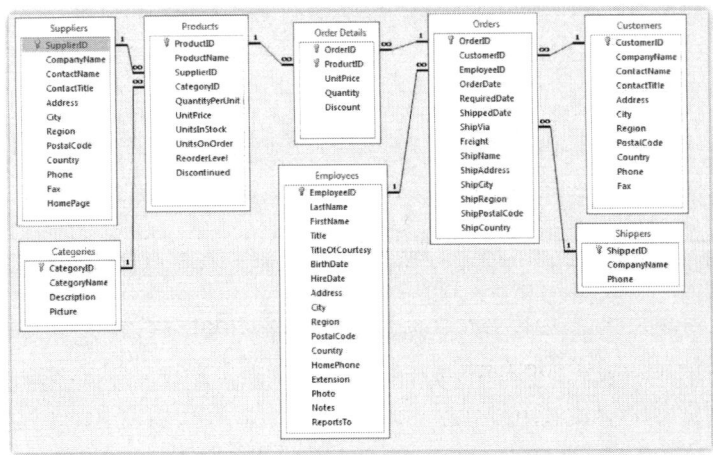

fg. 1 : Database schema of the Northwind Traders database

INTRODUCTION

> Terms displayed in ***bold italic*** can be found defined in the glossary on pg. 59.

What Is SQL?

Ideally, a database language must enable us to create structures, to perform data management chores (add, delete, modify) and to perform complex operations that transform the raw data into information. SQL, sometimes pronounced "sequel", is a support language for communicating with relational databases. SQL is also the language of choice for almost every RDBMS in use today because it provides a standardized method for storing and retrieving data. The SQL standard is maintained by both the American National Standards Institute (ANSI) and the International Standards Organization (ISO). The latest released version of the standard is SQL:2008 under ISO/IEC 9075. However, even with a standard in place there are numerous SQL dialects (PL/SQL, T-SQL, SQL-PL, MySQL) among the various vendors, evolving from requirements of the specific user community. This means that different RDBMS products implement SQL in slightly different ways.

SQL is a text-oriented language requiring only a text processor as it was developed long before graphical user interfaces. While todays' RDBMS products provide graphic tools for performing many SQL tasks, not everything can be done without delving into code. Additionally, SQL is quite different from procedural languages such as C++, Visual Basic and other languages where the programmer has to write step-by-step

> **NOTE**
>
> The SQL statements in this book run on Microsoft SQL Server and Microsoft Access. Running the SQL statements in a different RDBMS might require slight adjustments in some specific cases. Please refer to the documentation of the RDBMS of your personal choice.

Introduction

instructions to the computer in order to exactly define how to achieve a specified goal. SQL is a declarative language, which means that instead of using the language to tell the database what to do; you use it to tell the database what you want. With SQL you specify the results you want and the language itself determines the rest.

As discussed previously, a relational database is composed of tables that store data in a column/row format. At first glance, a database table resembles a spreadsheet with *rows* being your records and *columns* containing the fields for the records.

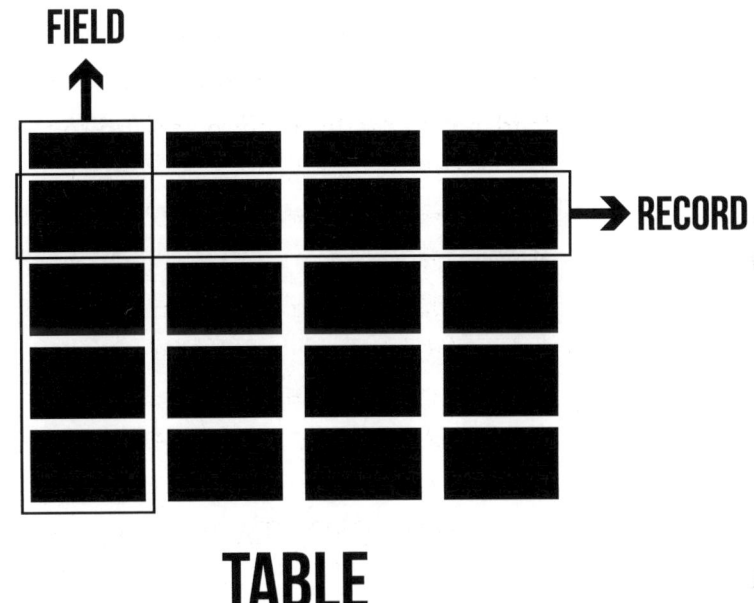

Each database management system tracks these tables by *indexing* them in a sort of data dictionary or catalog that contains a list of all the tables in the database. The list also stores pointers to each table's location. The dictionary can store additional metadata information as well, such as table definitions and even data specific to the database itself. When we send a request to the database using SQL, the database locates the requested table in the dictionary-without any additional instructions from our side. All we need to do is specify the name of the table, and the database will do the rest as SQL works independently of the internal structure of the database. The database then processes the request, called a *query*. For us a query is simply a question posed to the database. For the RDBMS a query is a SQL statement that must be executed.

SQL queries are the most common use of SQL. A query is a question we pose to the database, and the database then provides the data that answers our query. As databases store only raw data, just the facts without intelligence, we query the database with the purpose of processing the returned data and obtaining meaningful information. The broader definition of a query within the relational database environment is :

Que·ry *(n)* : A query is a statement written in SQL, which may include commands and actions, written to solicit an answer to a question or to perform an action.

Most SQL queries are used to answer questions such as "What products currently held in inventory are priced over $100 and what is the quantity on hand for each of those products?" or "How many employees have been hired by each of the company's departments since November 1, 2004?" We can think of a query as a type of sentence, with nouns, verbs, clauses, and predicates. For example, let's turn the following sentence into a query:

"Show me all the employees that live in the southwest region."

The subject in this case is the database, the verb is, "show me," the phrase "all the employees" is a clause, and "that live in the southwest region" is a ***predicate***. The resulting SQL statement resembles the following:

```
SELECT *
FROM Employees
WHERE Region = "Southwest"
```

Processing the request returns a table of data, which in SQL terms is called a view. A view can best be defined as a virtual table based on the parameters you passed to the database via your SQL statement.

In summary, a relational database model contains tables, each of which consists of a set of data. The data is structured into rows and columns, each row being a

> **NOTE**
>
> SQL Server is the name of a relational database management system that Microsoft distributes. SQL is a language. Therefore, SQL Server is not SQL. If you're unfamiliar with database systems and languages, it can be easy to confuse the two because the names are similar.

distinct *record*. To access the records in these tables you send requests to the database in the form of "queries" that are written in Structured Query Language (SQL). For the rest of this book you'll learn the basic SQL statements and syntax that you'll need to communicate with almost any relational database.

Syntax and Structure

In spoken languages, syntax dictates grammar and sentence structure. Similarly, in programming languages syntax dictates the structure and terminology to be used when writing code. In SQL, syntax is used to create statements as self-contained actions. Standard SQL is simple and straightforward as the bulk of the language is composed of commands, and learning how to arrange those commands in the proper order is all you really have to master. Because SQL's vocabulary is simple, SQL is relatively easy to learn with a basic command set vocabulary of less than 100 words. Also, as SQL is a nonprocedural language, we only have to command what is to be done and not worry about how it is going to be done.

There are three categories of SQL syntax term: identifiers, literals, and keywords. An identifier is a unique identifier for some element in a database system, such as a table, or a field name. If you create a database table called Customers, then 'Customers' is the identifier. A literal would be an actual data value like 'Edgar', '32', 'September 17, 2014'. A keyword is something that has meaning to the database system itself. It is a call to action with each keyword following its own rules on how to perform the action.

A SQL statement can be as simple as:

```
SELECT DateofBirth
FROM Customers
```

The above statement uses the keyword SELECT to select data from the field identified by the 'DateofBirth' name. The data is retrieved FROM the table identified by the 'Customers' name.

As we learn new keywords we will also learn what the database expects as a minimum and what options can be added to form a more prolific statement. Generally, SQL statements may be divided into the following categories:

- **Data Query Language (DQL)** : Statements that query the database but do not alter any data or database objects. This category contains the SELECT statement.

- **Data Manipulation Language (DML)** : Statements that modify data stored in database objects, such as tables. This category contains the INSERT, UPDATE, and DELETE statements.

- **Data Definition Language (DDL)** : Statements that create and modify database objects. Whereas DML and DQL work with the data in the database objects, DDL works with the database objects themselves. This category includes the CREATE, ALTER and DROP statements.

- **Data Control Language (DCL)** : Statements that manage privileges that database users have regarding the database objects. This category includes the GRANT and REVOKE statements.

The next chapter will present in detail how to use SQL as a data query language where we will learn the fundamentals of extracting information from the database. Afterwards, we will focus on SQL as a data manipulation language and learn how to insert, modify and delete. Finally, we will emphasize SQL as a data definition language as we delve into the core of databases and manipulate the database structure itself by defining and managing database objects.

CHAPTER ONE
Retrieving Data With SQL

SQL's most powerful feature is its ability to extract data. At a basic level, you can extract data in the same form in which it was originally entered into the database tables. Alternatively, you can query the database to obtain answers to questions that are not explicitly stated in the raw data. The key to retrieving data from a database is the SELECT statement. In its basic form the SELECT statement is very simple and easy to use. There are, however, many additional options that can make return more customized results.

The SELECT Statement

The most frequently used SQL statement is the SELECT statement. It is the workforce of the entire language. The SELECT statement retrieves data from the database for viewing in such a way so that it makes it easy to browse and analyze the data. Essentially, the SELECT statement is used to retrieve specific column(s) from a database table(s).

The SELECT statement can combine with five keyword clauses to specify and limit how the data from the table(s) is retrieved. The syntax looks something like this:

```
SELECT ColumnNames
FROM TableNames
[WHERE Condition]
[GROUP BY Column]
[HAVING Condition]
[ORDER BY Column][ASC | DESC]]
```

In this predefined syntax the FROM clause is the only keyword that is mandatory to combine with SELECT in order to retrieve data. The FROM statement is needed in order to specify to the database what tables in the database to retrieve the data from.

In the following examples we will start with the simplest form of the SELECT statement and add keyword clauses and literals to restrict the retrieval and/or presentation of the data. However, before we continue we must be aware of the general format conventions for SQL statements:

- Use uppercase for all keywords
- Most clauses appear on individual lines

In its simplest form, the SELECT statement retrieves all the columns from all the records in a table using just the mandatory FROM clause.

```
SELECT *
FROM Customers
```

The example above retrieves all the columns and records from the Customers table in the sample database. The resulting table might look something like **Figure 2**:

Customer I	Company Name	Contact Name	Contact Title	Address
ALFKI	Alfreds Futterkiste	Maria Anders	Sales Representative	Obere Str. 57
ANATR	Ana Trujillo Emparedados y helados	Ana Trujillo	Owner	Avda. de la Constitución 2222
ANTON	Antonio Moreno Taquería	Antonio Moreno	Owner	Mataderos 2312
AROUT	Around the Horn	Thomas Hardy	Sales Representative	120 Hanover Sq.
BERGS	Berglunds snabbköp	Christina Berglund	Order Administrator	Berguvsvägen 8
BLAUS	Blauer See Delikatessen	Hanna Moos	Sales Representative	Forsterstr. 57
BLONP	Blondel père et fils	Frédérique Citeaux	Marketing Manager	24, place Kléber
BOLID	Bólido Comidas preparadas	Martin Sommer	Owner	C/ Araquil, 67
BONAP	Bon app'	Laurence Lebihan	Owner	12, rue des Bouchers
BOTTM	Bottom-Dollar Markets	Elizabeth Lincoln	Accounting Manager	23 Tsawassen Blvd.
BSBEV	B's Beverages	Victoria Ashworth	Sales Representative	Fauntleroy Circus
CACTU	Cactus Comidas para llevar	Patricio Simpson	Sales Agent	Cerrito 333
CENTC	Centro comercial Moctezuma	Francisco Chang	Marketing Manager	Sierras de Granada 9993
CHOPS	Chop-suey Chinese	Yang Wang	Owner	Hauptstr. 29
COMMI	Comércio Mineiro	Pedro Afonso	Sales Associate	Av. dos Lusíadas, 23
CONSH	Consolidated Holdings	Elizabeth Brown	Sales Representative	Berkeley Gardens

fg. 2 : Result from a SELECT * statement

The asterisk character (*) is used as an argument in the SELECT clause to signify that all the columns from the underlying table must be retrieved. We should avoid using this shorthand unless we truly need all the columns; otherwise we are asking the database system to provide information we don't need, wasting processor power and memory. This might be insignificant when working with a small database but it makes a huge difference when many people are simultaneously accessing a large database.

The FROM Clause

The FROM clause specifies the tables from which the SELECT statement will retrieve data. This clause usually refers to one or more tables, but it can also include other queries. The following example for the FROM clause retrieves information from the Products table:

```
FROM Products
```

If you need to include information from more than one table, you separate the table names with commas:

```
FROM Products, Categories
```

If the table name consists of more than one word, then it has to be included in brackets ([]):

```
FROM Orders, [Order Details]
```

Limiting Data by Specifying Columns

The initial SELECT statement presented in this section used the asterisk (*) to retrieve all the data from the Customers table. However, we will seldom want to work with all the table data at one time. The first step to limiting data is to limit the retrieved columns by identifying only the columns you need. The syntax follows:

```
SELECT Column1, Column2...
FROM TableNames
```

When using this syntax, *we must* specify at least one column. If we include a list of columns, they have to be separated with a comma character just like the table names in the FROM clause. The following statement retrieves only three columns: *CustomerID*, *ContactName* and *ContactTitle*, from the *Customers* table **(Figure 3)**:

```
SELECT CustomerID, ContactName, ContactTitle
FROM Customers
```

Customer I	Contact Name	Contact Title
ALFKI	Maria Anders	Sales Representative
ANATR	Ana Trujillo	Owner
ANTON	Antonio Moreno	Owner
AROUT	Thomas Hardy	Sales Representative
BERGS	Christina Berglund	Order Administrator
BLAUS	Hanna Moos	Sales Representative
BLONP	Frédérique Citeaux	Marketing Manager
BOLID	Martín Sommer	Owner
BONAP	Laurence Lebihan	Owner
BOTTM	Elizabeth Lincoln	Accounting Manager
BSBEV	Victoria Ashworth	Sales Representative
CACTU	Patricio Simpson	Sales Agent
CENTC	Francisco Chang	Marketing Manager
CHOPS	Yang Wang	Owner
COMMI	Pedro Afonso	Sales Associate

fg. 3: SELECT results from the Customers table

The order in which the columns are listed in the SELECT statement determines the order in which the columns will be returned as results. The order of the results themselves usually reflects the order in which the records were entered into the database.

SQL Predicates

You can use predicates in combination with the SELECT statement to impose some limitations on the number of retrieved records. By default, the SELECT statement returns all records because SQL assumes that the ALL predicate is active. Therefore, using the statement:

```
SELECT ALL ContactName
FROM Customers
```

Is the same as using the following statement:

```
SELECT ContactName
FROM Customers
```

Returning DISTINCT rows

If you want to know all the unique values in a record and eliminate duplicate rows, you must use the DISTINCT predicate keyword. The DISTINCT keyword is added directly after the SELECT keyword to return a list of only unique data entries.

For example:

```
SELECT DISTINCT City
FROM Customers
```

Will return a unique list of cities from the Customers table, omitting the duplicates. This is essentially an answer to the question: "How many different cities do Customers come from?"

We are allowed to include additional columns in SELECT DISTINCT statements. While the additional columns will be considered, the elimination of duplicate values takes precedence from left to right. Therefore, additional columns will rarely have an effect on the values returned from the first column and should be used only if additional data is required, for example, if we needed to know the countries along with the cities (**Figure 4**).

```
SELECT DISTINCT City, Country
FROM Customers
```

City	Country
Aachen	Germany
Albuquerque	USA
Anchorage	USA
Århus	Denmark
Barcelona	Spain
Barquisimeto	Venezuela
Bergamo	Italy
Berlin	Germany
Bern	Switzerland
Boise	USA
Bräcke	Sweden
Brandenburg	Germany
Bruxelles	Belgium
Buenos Aires	Argentina

fg. 4: DISTINCT cities and countries for customers

In this case, the DISTINCT predicate discards records only if the combined values create a duplicate record. Only if a City with the same name exists in two countries will you get a duplicate value in the City field. Consequently, no duplicate results will be displayed if the City and the Country fields are both identical.

TOP

Another optional predicate keyword in the SELECT statement is the TOP keyword. TOP returns the top 'n' rows or top 'n' percent of records, based on the SELECT clause. This predicate is useful when you want to return a subset of records that meet all the other criteria. SQL processes the TOP predicate only after it completes all other criteria, such as joins, predicates, grouping, and sorts.

SQL QUICKSTART GUIDE

The TOP predicate uses the form:

```
TOP n [PERCENT] column1 [,column2...]
```

And can be combined with other predicates in the form:

```
SELECT [ALL | DISTINCT][TOP n
[PERCENT]column1[,column2...]]
```

Use TOP predicate to return the first 5 items from the Products table (**Figure 5**):

```
SELECT TOP 5 ProductID, ProductName, UnitPrice
FROM Products
```

Product I	Product Name	Unit Pric
1	Chai	$18.00
2	Chang	$19.00
3	Aniseed Syrup	$10.00
4	Chef Anton's Cajun Seasoning	$22.00
5	Chef Anton's Gumbo Mix	$21.35

fg. 5 : TOP 5 products as entered in the Products table

The query will return only five records. If instead you wanted to return five percent of the most expensive items, as opposed to just five records, you could use the following statement (**Figure 6**):

```
SELECT TOP 5 PERCENT ProductID, ProductName,
UnitPrice FROM Products
ORDER BY UnitPrice DESC
```

Product I	Product Name	Unit Pric
38	Côte de Blaye	$263.50
29	Thüringer Rostbratwurst	$123.79
9	Mishi Kobe Niku	$97.00
20	Sir Rodney's Marmalade	$81.00

fg. 6 : TOP 5 most expensive products as entered in the Products table

When working with percentages, the TOP predicate always rounds up to the next highest integer. Also, if the TOP predicate finds duplicate records that meet the SELECT statements criteria, it returns both records and includes them both in the count.

Most TOP queries simply don't make sense without the ORDER BY clause, since SQL returns what may seem like a meaningless set of records sorted by entry order. This clause will be reviewed later on.

> **NOTE**
>
> The syntax for the TOP predicate varies significantly across RDBMS. The examples above are valid only for Microsoft SQL Server and Microsoft Access.

The WHERE Clause

We will seldom have to select all of the records in a table. More often we will need to filter the results in order to obtain only the information we want. To accomplish this we can use the WHERE clause keyword in combination with the SELECT statement. Doing this, will set one or more conditions that must be fulfilled by a record before SQL includes that record in its results. The clause is used in the following syntax form:

```
SELECT data
FROM datasource
WHERE condition
```

The condition argument is stated as a conditional expression and can be as simple as a comparison to a given value or a complex expression. Let's start with a simple example that compares the data to a given value. The following statement returns only products that belong to the category with 1 as the ID value, the Beverage category.

The following statement returns only products with a selling price of over $10. (Figure 7).

```
SELECT ProductName, UnitPrice
FROM Products
WHERE UnitPrice > 10
```

Product Name	Unit Price
Chai	$18.00
Chang	$19.00
Chef Anton's Cajun Seasoning	$22.00
Chef Anton's Gumbo Mix	$21.35
Grandma's Boysenberry Spread	$25.00
Uncle Bob's Organic Dried Pears	$30.00
Northwoods Cranberry Sauce	$40.00
Mishi Kobe Niku	$97.00
Ikura	$31.00
Queso Cabrales	$21.00
Queso Manchego La Pastora	$38.00
Tofu	$23.25
Genen Shouyu	$15.50
Pavlova	$17.45
Alice Mutton	$39.00
Carnarvon Tigers	$62.50

fg. 7 : List of products costing more than $10

Comparison Operators

The conditions we use to filter records from a table usually involve comparing the values of an attribute to some constant value. We can ask whether the value of an attribute is the same, different, less than, or greater than some value. The response to the condition (ex. UnitPrice=10) is a statement or expression that is either true or false. As such, comparisons are also called Boolean expressions. The most common *comparison operators* are presented in **Table 1**.

OPERATOR	MEANING
=	Equal To
>	Greater Than
<	Less Than
>=	Greater Than or Equal To
<=	Less Than or Equal To
<>	Not Equal To

Table. 1 : List of conditional operators

Comparisons can be done between numbers (numerical), text (alphabetical) and dates (chronological). Comparing numbers is straightforward, but when comparing text attributes, the values have to be put in a character field within quotation marks (""). For example, the following query will return all companies that are not from Berlin **(Figure 8)**.

```
SELECT CompanyName
FROM Customers
WHERE City <> "Berlin"
```

Text comparison is alphabetical, meaning that "A" comes before "Z", so "A" < "Z". Putting numbers in a character field will filter the results alphabetically "40" < "5" and vice versa, putting text in number fields will filter the results numerically. We have to make sure we are using the correct type, or we might end up with some surprising query results.

Comparison operators can also be used with date/time values. Instead of using quotation marks, we enclose the date/time values in pound signs (##). **Table 2** gives a list of possible date conditions that can appear in a WHERE clause. Comparison operators allow for many different queries with which we can compare a value of an identifier with a literal (ex. Country = "Germany").

Company Name
Ana Trujillo Emparedados y helados
Antonio Moreno Taquería
Around the Horn
Berglunds snabbköp
Blauer See Delikatessen
Blondel père et fils
Bólido Comidas preparadas
Bon app'
Bottom-Dollar Markets
B's Beverages
Cactus Comidas para llevar
Centro comercial Moctezuma
Chop-suey Chinese
Comércio Mineiro
Consolidated Holdings

CONDITION	MEANING
OrderDate =#19/7/1996#	Orders made **on** July 19th, 1996
OrderDate <#19/7/1996#	Orders made **before** July 19th, 1996
OrderDate >#19/7/1996#	Orders made **after** July 19th, 1996
OrderDate >=#1/1/1996# AND OrderDate <=#31/12/1996#	Orders made **in** July

fg. 8 : List of companies not situated in Berlin

Table. 2 : Using conditional operators with dates

NOTE

When comparing text, some implementations of SQL are case-sensitive while others are not. For situations in which the SQL implementation is case-sensitive and you need to retrieve data by disregarding the case of the letters, use the function UPPER to turn the value of each text attribute into uppercase before the comparison takes place (ex. WHERE UPPER (Country) = "GERMANY").

Logical Operators

When more than one condition needs to be tested in a WHERE statement, we can use the NOT, AND, and OR *logical operators* to link the conditions. The meaning of these operators is synonymous with their meaning in the English language; the NOT operator means that the condition(s) must be false, the AND operator means that all listed conditions need to be true, and the OR operator indicates that only one of the conditions needs to be true. Adding criteria complicates the WHERE clause but gives us more control over the results.

As an example, the following query will return all products that cost more than $10 but less than $100. **(Figure 9)**.

```
SELECT ProductName, UnitPrice
FROM Products
WHERE UnitPrice >=10
AND UnitPrice <=100
```

The NOT operator is used to negate the result of a conditional expression. In SQL, all expressions evaluate to true and false. If the expression is true, the row is selected; if it is false, it is discarded. Therefore, the NOT operator is used to find the rows *that do not match* a certain condition. In essence, including the NOT operator will cause the query to return the opposite results of a standard query **(Figure 10)**. In the following example, the query selects all suppliers that come neither from France nor the USA:

```
SELECT CompanyName, Country
FROM Suppliers
WHERE NOT Country = "France"
AND NOT Country = "USA"
```

Product Name	Unit Pric
Chai	$18.00
Chang	$19.00
Aniseed Syrup	$10.00
Chef Anton's Cajun Seasoning	$22.00
Chef Anton's Gumbo Mix	$21.35
Grandma's Boysenberry Spread	$25.00
Uncle Bob's Organic Dried Pears	$30.00
Northwoods Cranberry Sauce	$40.00
Mishi Kobe Niku	$97.00
Ikura	$31.00
Queso Cabrales	$21.00
Queso Manchego La Pastora	$38.00
Tofu	$23.25
Genen Shouyu	$15.50
Pavlova	$17.45

fg. 9 : List of products costing between $10 and $100

Company Name	Country
Exotic Liquids	UK
Tokyo Traders	Japan
Cooperativa de Quesos 'Las Cabras'	Spain
Mayumi's	Japan
Pavlova, Ltd.	Australia
Specialty Biscuits, Ltd.	UK
PB Knäckebröd AB	Sweden
Refrescos Americanas LTDA	Brazil
Heli Süßwaren GmbH & Co. KG	Germany
Plutzer Lebensmittelgroßmärkte AG	Germany
Nord-Ost-Fisch Handelsgesellschaft mb	Germany
Formaggi Fortini s.r.l.	Italy
Norske Meierier	Norway
Svensk Sjöföda AB	Sweden
Leka Trading	Singapore

fg. 10 : List of suppliers that exclude France and USA

The WHERE clause is flexible. We can refer to columns that aren't in the SELECT clause-as long, as those columns are present in the referenced tables. For example, let's suppose that we want to see a list of suppliers that are either from Brazil or are situated in Tokyo **(Figure 11)**. The following statement uses an OR operator to include both conditions in one WHERE clause without including the condition columns in the results.

```
SELECT CompanyName
FROM Suppliers
WHERE Country = "Brazil" OR City = "Tokyo"
```

fg. 11 : List of suppliers coming from the country of Brazil or the city of Tokyo

NOTE

The case-sensitivity of some SQL implementations are also present when using the LIKE operator (ex. LIKE M% would be different from LIKE m%).

Dealing With Ranges and Wildcards

The BETWEEN operator allows us to specify a range between one value and another. In a previous example, to check for a value within a certain range we used the "greater than or equal to" (>=) and the "less than or equal to" (<=) operators. The BETWEEN operator functions in exactly the same way with the end points of the range included in the condition. So instead of writing:

```
WHERE UnitPrice >=5
AND <=100
```

You can write:

```
WHERE UnitPrice
BETWEEN 5 AND 100
```

The BETWEEN operator can be used in conjunction with other data types, such as text and dates.

When searching for partial values, SQL provides the LIKE operator, which compares field values to a specified pattern. While creating the pattern you can use wildcard characters to replace unknown characters. A wildcard character doesn't match a specific character, but instead matches any one or any of more characters. The underscore (_) replaces one unknown value, while the percentage symbol (%) replaces any number of unknown values.

The following example lists all products for which the price has 1 as the first digit and any other number as a second digit **(Figure 12)**.

```
SELECT ProductName, UnitPrice
FROM Products
WHERE UnitPrice LIKE "1?"
```

> **NOTE**
>
> Microsoft Access uses the asterisk (*) instead of percentage (%) and the question mark (?) instead of the underscore (_).

Product Name	Unit Price
Chai	$18.00
Chang	$19.00
Aniseed Syrup	$10.00
Sir Rodney's Scones	$10.00
NuNuCa Nuß-Nougat-Creme	$14.00
Sasquatch Ale	$14.00
Steeleye Stout	$18.00
Inlagd Sill	$19.00
Chartreuse verte	$18.00
Singaporean Hokkien Fried Mee	$14.00
Spegesild	$12.00
Louisiana Hot Spiced Okra	$17.00
Laughing Lumberjack Lager	$14.00
Outback Lager	$15.00
Röd Kaviar	$15.00
Longlife Tofu	$10.00
Lakkalikööri	$18.00
Original Frankfurter grüne Soße	$13.00

fg. 12 : List of products costing 10 and something dollars

The following example **(Figure. 13)** displays all companies that come from a country beginning with the letter F.

```
SELECT CompanyName
FROM Customers
WHERE Country LIKE "F*"
```

Company Name
Blondel père et fils
Bon app'
Du monde entier
Folies gourmandes
France restauration
La corne d'abondance
La maison d'Asie
Paris spécialités
Spécialités du monde
Victuailles en stock
Vins et alcools Chevalier
Wartian Herkku
Wilman Kala

fg. 13 : List of companies in countries beginning with the letter F

Operator Precedence

When there is more than one operator in a condition, there are certain rules that determine the order in which operators are evaluated. A hierarchy of operators will determine which operator is evaluated first when the condition contains multiple operators. The highest precedence is given to brackets ([]), followed by the NOT operator, the AND operator and all of the following operators with the same precedence: ALL, ANY, BETWEEN, IN, LIKE, OR, and SOME.

Additionally:
- If the operators have different precedence, then the highest ones are evaluated first, then the next highest, and so on.
- If all the operators have equal precedence, then the conditions are interpreted from left to right.

Technically, the best way to ensure operator precedence is to use brackets. They can make the SQL easier to read because by making it clear which conditions are evaluated first, which is quite helpful when the conditions are complex.

The ORDER BY Clause

Up to this point query results have come in the order the database decides, usually based on the order in which the data was entered (except for the example used in the TOP keyword description.) Listing query results in a specific order is a frequent requirement, which in SQL is specified with the ORDER BY clause keyword. The ORDER BY clause goes at the very end of the SELECT statement, after the WHERE clause, and defines the column(s) that will determine either the ascending or the descending order of the results.

The following example (**Figure 14**) sorts customers by the name of the company. SQL will perform an alphabetic sort, since CompanyName is a text column.

```
SELECT CompanyName, ContactName, ContactTitle, City
FROM Customers
ORDER BY CompanyName
```

Company Name	Contact Name	Contact Title	City
Alfreds Futterkiste	Maria Anders	Sales Representative	Berlin
Ana Trujillo Emparedados y helados	Ana Trujillo	Owner	México D.F.
Antonio Moreno Taquería	Antonio Moreno	Owner	México D.F.
Around the Horn	Thomas Hardy	Sales Representative	London
Berglunds snabbköp	Christina Berglund	Order Administrator	Luleå
Blauer See Delikatessen	Hanna Moos	Sales Representative	Mannheim
Blondel père et fils	Frédérique Citeaux	Marketing Manager	Strasbourg
Bólido Comidas preparadas	Martín Sommer	Owner	Madrid
Bon app'	Laurence Lebihan	Owner	Marseille
Bottom-Dollar Markets	Elizabeth Lincoln	Accounting Manager	Tsawassen
B's Beverages	Victoria Ashworth	Sales Representative	London

fg. 14: Alphabetical list of companies

ORDER BY will sort the records into ascending order by default, which is evident from the results of the preceding SQL sort from A to Z. If you require descending order, you must add DESC after the list of columns in the ORDER BY clause. For example, the following statement sorts the results of the query in a descending order by CompanyName.

```
SELECT CompanyName, ContactName, ContactTitle, City
FROM Customers
ORDER BY CompanyName DESC
```

Company Name	Contact Name	Contact Title	City
Wolski Zajazd	Zbyszek Piestrzeniewicz	Owner	Warszawa
Wilman Kala	Matti Karttunen	Owner/Marketing Assistant	Helsinki
White Clover Markets	Karl Jablonski	Owner	Seattle
Wellington Importadora	Paula Parente	Sales Manager	Resende
Wartian Herkku	Pirkko Koskitalo	Accounting Manager	Oulu
Vins et alcools Chevalier	Paul Henriot	Accounting Manager	Reims
Victuailles en stock	Mary Saveley	Sales Agent	Lyon
Vaffeljernet	Palle Ibsen	Sales Manager	Århus
Trail's Head Gourmet Provisioners	Helvetius Nagy	Sales Associate	Kirkland
Tradição Hipermercados	Anabela Domingues	Sales Representative	São Paulo
Tortuga Restaurante	Miguel Angel Paolino	Owner	México D.F.

fg. 15: Alphabetical list of companies presented in a descending order

Because ascending order is the default for ORDER BY, specifying ascending order is not necessary in the SQL query. Additionally, the column used to order the results doesn't have to form part of the results. Furthermore, we can use more than one column to sort results by simply listing each column by which to sort the results and separating each column with a comma. The order in which the columns are defined in the SELECT statement will determine the order of priority in sorting. For example, the following statement sorts the results of the query in a descending order by ContactTitle and then each group of records containing the same ContactTitle is further sorted by city in an ascending order. **(Figure 16)**.

```
SELECT CompanyName, ContactName, ContactTitle, City
FROM Customers
ORDER BY ContactTitle DESC, City
```

Company Name	Contact Name	Contact Title	City
Old World Delicatessen	Rene Phillips	Sales Representative	Anchorage
Alfreds Futterkiste	Maria Anders	Sales Representative	Berlin
Save-a-lot Markets	Jose Pavarotti	Sales Representative	Boise
Rancho grande	Sergio Gutiérrez	Sales Representative	Buenos Aires
Hungry Coyote Import Store	Yoshi Latimer	Sales Representative	Elgin
Lehmanns Marktstand	Renate Messner	Sales Representative	Frankfurt a.M.
Princesa Isabel Vinhos	Isabel de Castro	Sales Representative	Lisboa
Consolidated Holdings	Elizabeth Brown	Sales Representative	London
B's Beverages	Victoria Ashworth	Sales Representative	London
Around the Horn	Thomas Hardy	Sales Representative	London
Blauer See Delikatessen	Hanna Moos	Sales Representative	Mannheim

fg. 16 : List of companies ordered by multiple columns

Using Aliases with the AS Clause

When retrieving columns from the database tables, you are not limited to just using column names. If necessary you can give column names *aliases* in the results where the aliases would simply be secondary names for collections of data. For example, if you want your results to display an alias called Surname instead of the predefined field name LastName, you can write the following query.

```
SELECT LastName AS Surname
FROM Employees
```

Using an alias doesn't change the results returned in any way, nor does it rename the LastName column from the Customers table. By combining the SELECT statement with an AS clause, you essentially create a temporary name for a column or a group of columns. This clause is optional, and when it is omitted, SQL uses the default column's name.

With aliases you can also combine the data from two or more columns into one column, with the resulting column bearing the alias name. The joining of columns is also known as concatenation, which as an approach varies depending on the RDBMS. In Microsoft SQL Server and MS Access you use the concatenation operator, which is the plus (+) sign.

The following query **(Figure 17)** will join the FirstName and LastName columns into a new alias column called FullName.

```
SELECT FirstName + LastName AS FullName
FROM Employees
```

FullName
NancyDavolio
AndrewFuller
JanetLeverling
MargaretPeacock
StevenBuchanan
MichaelSuyama
RobertKing
LauraCallahan
AnneDodsworth

fg. 17

Full Name
NancyDavolio
AndrewFuller
JanetLeverling
MargaretPeacock
StevenBuchanan
MichaelSuyama
RobertKing
LauraCallahan
AnneDodsworth

fg. 18

fg. 17 : Example of concatenating columns in a single alias column

fg. 18 : Example of concatenating columns in a single alias column with space.

Obviously, the results are slightly lacking as our intent was not to glue the two columns together, but to have them as two separate words placed into one column. **(Figure 18)** Hence, we need to include the empty space between the concatenated columns in the SQL query itself. Hence, our statement should be structured as follows:

```
SELECT FirstName + " " + LastName AS FullName
FROM Employees
```

Selecting Records from Multiple Tables

Until this point the SQL queries we used were extracting data from only one database table. This is quite limiting, as answers usually require the joining of data from more than one table. To understand why *joins* are useful, let's suppose that we want a list of products from the "Beverages" category **(Figure 19)**. If we just use the following statement:

```
SELECT Products.ProductName, Categories.CategoryName
FROM Categories, Products
```

Product Name	Category Name
Chai	Beverages
Chai	Condiments
Chai	Confections
Chai	Dairy Products
Chai	Grains/Cereals
Chai	Meat/Poultry
Chai	Produce
Chai	Seafood
Chang	Beverages
Chang	Condiments
Chang	Confections
Chang	Dairy Products

fg. 19 : Retrieving products results from 2 tables

The SQL query will return all the possible combinations of records from the Categories and Products tables, which is obviously not the required result. If we take a closer look at the Products table we will see that there is only a numerical value for CategoryID, while the name corresponding to that numerical value has to be looked up in the Categories table. However, in SQL the tables are combined using the **join operation**. If SQL didn't support joins, we would have to first determine that the CategoryID value for "Beverages" is 1 and then use this information in the WHERE clause.

In the example above, since it was not explicitly stated, the join operation was performed on all fields, because there were no guidelines as to how to combine the two tables. As the link has been identified, we will use what is known as an inner join to combine the two tables. The inner join will allow us to specify the columns and the originating tables that form the join and under what conditions. For example, we can specify a condition that says the CategoryID field from the Categories table is equivalent to the CategoryID field from the Products

NOTE

Since the query retrieves data from multiple tables, the field name in the SELECT statement must be preceded with the table name. Otherwise, there would be no way of distinguishing between two fields from different tables if those filed share the same name.

table. Only records with a matching CategoryID in both tables will be included in the final results.

The syntax for inner join follows the following structure:

```
Table1 INNER JOIN table2 ON column_from_table1 = column_from_table2
```

The SELECT statement expectantly begins with a list of the columns required to form the results. The FROM line doesn't just list the tables used in the query, but this time the INNER JOIN keyword is used to specify that the two tables should be joined. The ON keyword that follows specifics what joins the tables, which in this case is the CategoryID field from both tables **(Figure 20)**. Applying the syntax to our situation yields the following code:

```
SELECT Products.ProductName, Categories.CategoryName
FROM Categories INNER JOIN Products ON Categories.CategoryID=Products.CategoryID
WHERE Categories.CategoryName = "Beverages"
```

fg. 20 : Retrieving products results from inner joined tables

Product Name	Category Nam
Chai	Beverages
Chang	Beverages
Guaraná Fantástica	Beverages
Sasquatch Ale	Beverages
Steeleye Stout	Beverages
Côte de Blaye	Beverages
Chartreuse verte	Beverages
Ipoh Coffee	Beverages
Laughing Lumberjack Lager	Beverages
Outback Lager	Beverages
Rhönbräu Klosterbier	Beverages
Lakkalikööri	Beverages

NOTE

Only Microsoft Access requires the INNER keyword when performing a join. For other RDBM's the INNER keyword is omitted and only the JOIN... ON syntax is used.

Using INNER JOIN or simply JOIN to create an inner join between tables is not the only way to join tables. An alternative way to define a relationship between the tables by connecting the contents of two fields is simply to specify the link in the WHERE clause. This would restructure the previous SQL statement as follows:

```
SELECT Products.ProductName, Categories.CategoryName
FROM Categories, Products
WHERE Categories.CategoryID=Products.CategoryID
AND Categories.CategoryName = "Beverages"
```

In this case the WHERE clause specifies that Categories.CategoryID should equal Products.CategoryID, which creates the join. Technically, this yields the same results as INNER JOIN. However, it is considered that INNER JOIN makes an explicit statement as to which tables are joined making the SQL easier to read and understand. When using joins we are not limited to only joining two tables. As a matter of fact, it is possible to join as many tables as the desired information requires. For example, let's suppose we want a list of suppliers of beverage products with each product listed along with the product price. When we want to design more complex queries, we first have to work out what information is required and how it is connected across tables. If we look at the database tables it is easy to identify that we will need four data items: CompanyName, ProductName, UnitPrice, CategoryName from three different tables: Products, Categories and Suppliers. We can also identify that the Categories and Products tables are connected by the CategoryID field while the Suppliers and Products tables are connected by the SupplierID field **(Figure 21)**. With this we have enough information to construct the SQL statement as follows.

```
SELECT Products.ProductName, Categories.CategoryName, Products.UnitPrice, Suppliers.CompanyName
FROM Categories INNER JOIN Products ON Categories.CategoryID=Products.CategoryID INNER JOIN Suppliers ON Products.SupplierID=Suppliers.SupplierID
WHERE Categories.CategoryName = "Beverages"
```

Product Name	Company Name	Category Nam
Chai	Exotic Liquids	Beverages
Chang	Exotic Liquids	Beverages
Guaraná Fantástica	Refrescos Americanas LTDA	Beverages
Sasquatch Ale	Bigfoot Breweries	Beverages
Steeleye Stout	Bigfoot Breweries	Beverages
Côte de Blaye	Aux joyeux ecclésiastiques	Beverages
Chartreuse verte	Aux joyeux ecclésiastiques	Beverages
Ipoh Coffee	Leka Trading	Beverages
Laughing Lumberjack Lager	Bigfoot Breweries	Beverages
Outback Lager	Pavlova, Ltd.	Beverages
Rhönbräu Klosterbier	Plutzer Lebensmittelgroßmärkte AG	Beverages
Lakkalikööri	Karkki Oy	Beverages

fg. 21 : Retrieving products results from multiple inner joined tables

Including Excluded Data with OUTER JOIN

In some occasions, situations arise in which the INNER JOIN examples from the previous section would discard potentially useful data. For instance, if a product has no category assigned to it, then it would never be returned as a valid result since the condition Category.CategoryID=Products.CategoryID is not fulfilled. This kind of loss is not always desirable, so there is a special type of join called an outer join to deal with these situations. Before we explain outer joins, let's give them a different perspective in order to understand joins better.

With trickier queries, especially those involving more than one table, thinking in terms of sets of records can be helpful. Let's view each table in the database as a set of records. When we run a SQL query, the results can also be viewed as a set of records. Hence, the following two queries will result into two different sets of records that contain all records from their respective tables. **(Figure 22 & 23)**.

```
SELECT Products.ProductName, UnitPrice
FROM Products
SELECT Categories.CategoryName
FROM Categories
```

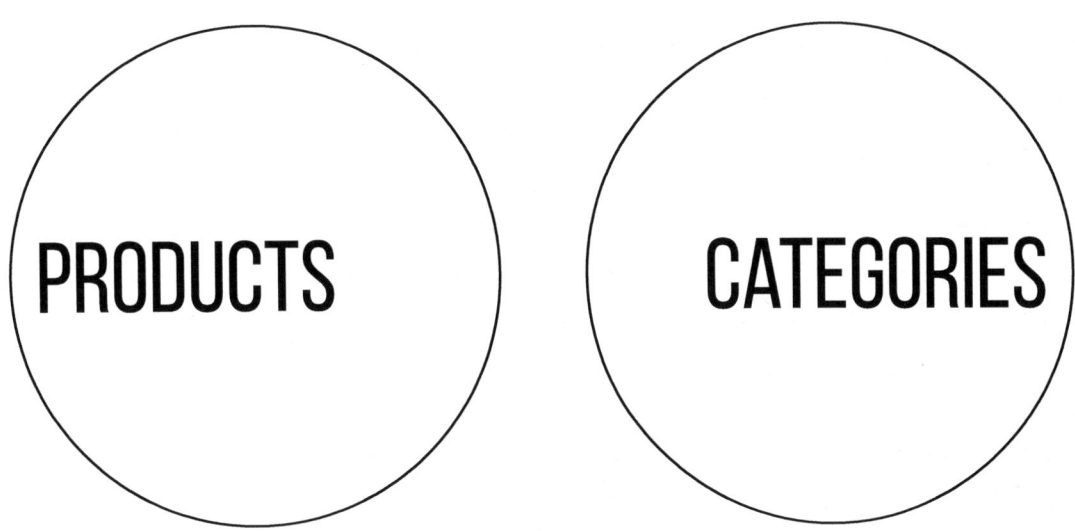

fg. 22 : Presenting table data as sets

When we join these sets of records with an INNER JOIN (Figure 23), we essentially include only those records in which there is an overlap as defined by the ON clause.

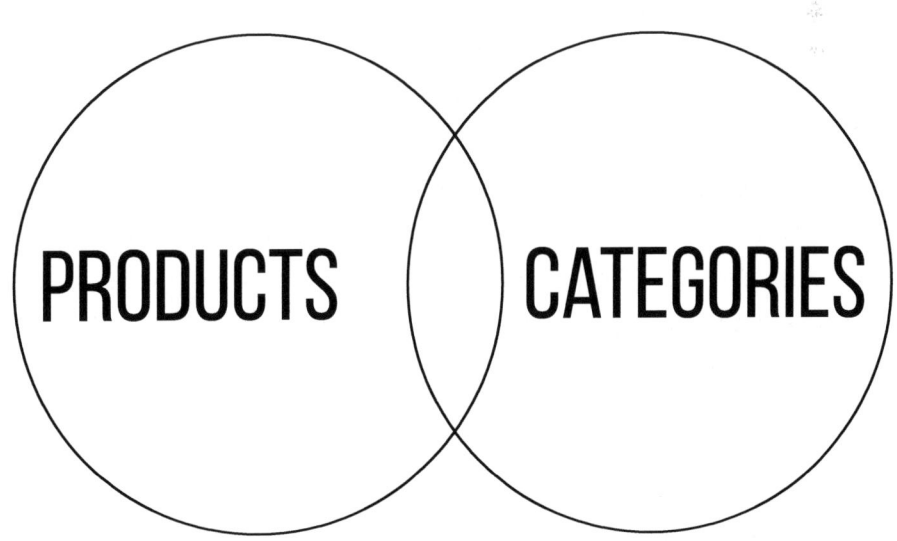

fg. 23 : Overlapping sets with INNER JOIN

SQL QUICKSTART GUIDE

An inner join requires that both sets of records involved in the join include matching records. If we want to include records from either side of the sets that are not overlapping, we need to use an outer join. An outer join doesn't require a match on both sides, as we can specify which table will always return results regardless of the conditions in the ON clause. There are three types of outer joins: left outer join, right outer join, and full outer join. The syntax is identical to that for inner joins; the only change is the OUTER JOIN keyword.

In a left outer join, all the records from the table named on the left of the OUTER JOIN statement are returned, regardless of whether there is a matching record in the table on the right of the OUTER JOIN statement. For example **(Figure 24)**, the following query:

```
SELECT Products.ProductName, Categories.CategoryName
FROM Categories LEFT OUTER JOIN Products
ON Categories.CategoryID=Products.CategoryID
```

Product Name	Category Name
Spegesild	Seafood
Escargots de Bourgogne	Seafood
Röd Kaviar	Seafood
	Vegetables

fg. 24 : Product results from a LEFT OUTER JOIN example

Will also return categories for which no products are defined. Conversely, in a **right outer join**, all the records from the table named on the right of the OUTER JOIN statement are returned, regardless of whether there is a matching record in the table on the left of the OUTER JOIN statement **(Figure 25)**. For example, the following query:

```
SELECT Products.ProductName, Categories.CategoryName
FROM Categories RIGHT OUTER JOIN Products
ON Categories.CategoryID=Products.CategoryID
```

Product Name	Category Name
Scottish Porridge	
Kongee	
Chai	Beverages
Chang	Beverages
Guaraná Fantástica	Beverages
Sasquatch Ale	Beverages
Steeleye Stout	Beverages
Côte de Blaye	Beverages
Chartreuse verte	Beverages
Ipoh Coffee	Beverages
Laughing Lumberjack Lager	Beverages

fg. 25 : Products results from a RIGHT OUTER JOIN example

Will also return products that don't have a category assigned to them. The full outer join is essentially a combination of left and right outer joins. Records from both the table on the left and right are included even if there are no matching records. Many database systems don't support this join, and neither MS Access nor MySQL offer any alternatives.

NULL Values

What values are contained in fields in which no value is specified? Logically, database fields with no values are empty fields, but SQL doesn't allow for data to hold no value. As a matter of fact, fields with no specified value are considered NULL. NULL is not the same as nothing; it represents the unknown. When we don't enter data into a database cell, SQL considers that there is a value that one day might be known and stored in this field, but at this moment that value is unknown. That is where NULL comes into the picture.

Why should we care about all this? Well, unknown values, or NULLs, can lead to unexpected and overlooked results. For example, you might consider that the following SQL would return all the records from the Employees table:

```
SELECT FirstName, LastName, BirthDate
FROM Employees
WHERE BirthDate >= #1800-01-01#
```

However, if there is an employee for whom the BirthDate field was omitted during data entry, the name of that employee will not appear in the results. In order to check for NULL values, we must use the IS NULL operator **(Figure 26)**.

```
SELECT FirstName, LastName, BirthDate
FROM Employees
WHERE BirthDate >= #1800-01-01# OR BirthDate
IS NULL
```

First Name	Last Name	Birth Date
Nancy	Davolio	08-Dec-1968
Andrew	Fuller	
Janet	Leverling	30-Aug-1963
Margaret	Peacock	19-Sep-1958
Steven	Buchanan	04-Mar-1955
Michael	Suyama	02-Jul-1963
Robert	King	29-May-1960
Laura	Callahan	09-Jan-1958
Anne	Dodsworth	02-Jul-1969

fg. 26 : Querying null data

Generally, it is better to avoid the NULL value whenever possible and, if possible, assign a default value to the field during data entry.

CHAPTER TWO
Built-In Functions and Arithmetic Calculations

The SQL queries we have used so far return results as a set of individual records. If instead we want to summarize the records' data (ex. find the average price), we need to provide an aggregation of results. SQL has many ***aggregate functions*** for manipulating numbers and text, both basic and advanced, and it allows for calculations of values based on table data **(Table 3)**.

SQL includes five built-in functions:

FUNCTION	MEANING
COUNT	Counts the number of rows in results
SUM	Totals the set of values in a numeric column
AVG	Averages the set of values in a numeric column
MIN	Selects the row with the minimum value
MAX	Selects the row with the maximum value

Table. 3 : SQL built-in functions

COUNT

The COUNT function is used to count the number of records that are returned as a result of a query. It is used in the SELECT statement along with the column name for which the counting is to take place. The value returned in the results set is the number of non-empty values in that column. Alternatively, instead of a column name you can insert an asterisk (*), in which case all columns for all records in the results will be counted.

For example, **(Figure 27)**, if we want to count the number of Products in our database, we use the following query:

```
SELECT COUNT(*)
FROM Products
```

Or

```
SELECT COUNT(ProductID)
FROM Products
```

fg. 27 : Counting products

[Expr1000: 79]

In the COUNT function the actual column name is not as important as long as it is a field that can be counted towards the requested result. Usually, the smartest approach is to count the ID fields in a table, as these fields are least likely to be empty.

It is possible to include more than one function in the SELECT statement **(Figure 28)**. For example, the following statement returns the number of non-empty CompanyName fields and non-empty Fax fields.

```
SELECT COUNT (CompanyName), COUNT (Fax)
FROM Customers
```

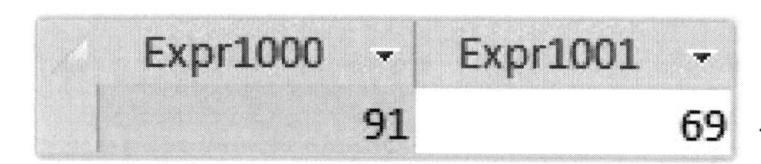

[Expr1000: 91 | Expr1001: 69]

fg. 28 : Counting more than one column

However, combining a function with a regular column will result in an error (ex. SELECT Phone, COUNT(CompanyName). In these cases the identifier will return more than one row of results, whereas COUNT always returns only one row.

In the above COUNT example, **(Figure 28)**, it is noticeable that the retrieved result is placed inside a column with a system-generated name. To define a column name we can use alias names with the AS clause **(Figure 29)**.

```
SELECT COUNT(ProductID) AS NumberOfProducts
FROM Products
```

[NumberOfProduct: 79]

fg. 29 : Counting with alias column names

SUM

The SUM function adds up all the values for the expression passed to it as an argument. The expression itself can be a column name or a calculation and can only be performed with numerical fields. As an example let's use a numerical column to calculate the total items we have in stock.

```
SELECT SUM(UnitsInStock)
FROM Products
```

Another more logical example would be to calculate the total income from all items sold **(Figure 30)**. For this query we need to use the Order Details table from which we will calculate the sum of UnitPrice*Quantity*Discount.

```
SELECT SUM(UnitPrice * Quantity * Discount)
FROM [Order Details]
```

fg. 30 : Summing data from multiple column expressions

Just like with the COUNT example, the retrieved result is placed inside a system-generated column. To define a column name we can define an alias with the AS keyword.

```
SELECT SUM(UnitPrice * Quantity * Discount)
AS TotalIncome
FROM [Order Details]
```

Other Functions

The AVG function takes the total sum of values in the expression and divides that value by the number of rows. The expression, whether it is a specific column or a calculation, must have a numeric value in order to return a valid result. For example, let's say that we want to check the average product price in our store database:

```
SELECT AVG (UnitPrice)
FROM Products
```

Of course, as with other functions and queries, we can use alias columns and aggregate data from multiple tables **(Figure 31)**. The following query calculates the average price of beverage products.

```
SELECT AVG (UnitPrice) AS AverageBeveragePrice
FROM Products INNER JOIN Categories
ON Products.CategoryID=Categories.CategoryID
WHERE CategoryName = "Beverages"
```

AverageBeveragePrice
$37.98

fg. 31 : Average price for beverages

The MAX and MIN functions return the highest and the lowest values that can be found in the resulting record set. These functions can be used with non-numeric data types, unlike the SUM and AVG functions. For example, we can use MAX and MIN to find the youngest and oldest employees by determining the earliest and latest dates of birth. **(Figure 32)**.

```
SELECT MAX(BirthDate), MIN(BirthDate)
FROM Employees
```

Expr1000	Expr1001
7/2/1969	3/4/1955

fg. 32 : Oldest and youngest employees

Additionally, we can also calculate the largest and smallest value in a character field. This means that MAX will return the alphabetically largest value, as close to the letter Z as possible, while MIN will return the alphabetically lowest value closest to the letter A.

```
SELECT MAX(LastName), MIN(LastName)
FROM Employees
```

Grouping Data with the GROUP BY Clause

Now that we have started summarizing the data, we can start using groups in order to provide more detailed and refined data aggregation. With grouping we can find out more information about a particular record in accordance with specific parameters.

The GROUP BY clause defines groups that you might want to evaluate in some calculation as a whole. Used in conjunction with the SELECT statement, the GROUP BY clause allows us to group identical data into one subset instead of listing each individual record. From a syntax perspective, the GROUP BY clause always goes after any FROM or WHERE clauses in the SELECT statement, with all the columns we want to be grouped included in the column list.

Let's say that we want to find out the countries from which our customers come. Using the GROUP BY clause, we would write the following query:

```
SELECT Country
FROM Customers
GROUP BY Country
```

As the answer doesn't require a list of every member and the state in which each member lives, with the GROUP BY clause we simply ask SQL to treat the customers who come from the same state as one data instance.

If we want to include more than one column in the GROUP BY clause, then we separate the columns with commas, the same way we separate columns in other clauses. Following on the previous example, if we also want to know the cities in which our customers live, we will use the following query:

```
SELECT City, Country
FROM Customers
GROUP BY City, Country
```

Notice that **Figure 33 & Figure 34** include the same columns both in the SELECT statement and the GROUP BY clause. Most RDBMSs will not allow the columns to be different, because if we don't specify a group for a column in the SELECT statement, then there is no way of deciding which value to include for a particular group. The results can include only one identical record per group, and each row represents the results from a group of records, not the individual records themselves. Including an ungrouped column will create more than one row for each group, which isn't allowed.

The GROUP BY clause is at its most powerful when combined with SQL's summarizing and aggregating functions. As the GROUP BY clause doesn't actually summarize data, any calculations for summarizing that data must be provided in the form of built-in functions.

If we build on the previous example, and instead of a list of countries we want to know how many customers come from each country based on the information from the Customers table, we can use the following query:

```
SELECT Country,
COUNT(CustomerID)
FROM Customers
GROUP BY Country
```

City	Country
Aachen	Germany
Albuquerque	USA
Anchorage	USA
Århus	Denmark
Barcelona	Spain
Barquisimeto	Venezuela
Bergamo	Italy
Berlin	Germany
Bern	Switzerland
Boise	USA
Bräcke	Sweden
Brandenburg	Germany
Bruxelles	Belgium
Buenos Aires	Argentina
Butte	USA
Campinas	Brazil
Caracas	Venezuela
Charleroi	Belgium
Cork	Ireland
Cowes	UK
Cunewalde	Germany

fg. 33: Results for cities from the GROUP BY example query

Going back to our first COUNT example, we counted the total number of items in the Products table. With the GROUP BY clause we can now identify the number of products per category. As we will be retrieving data from more than one table, we will also use a join as well as an alias for the results of the COUNT function.

```
SELECT Categories.
CategoryName,
COUNT (Products.ProductID)
AS NumberOfProducts
FROM Categories
INNER JOIN Products
ON Categories.CategoryID=
Products.CategoryID
GROUP BY Categories.
CategoryName
```

Country	Expr1001
Argentina	3
Austria	2
Belgium	2
Brazil	9
Canada	3
Denmark	2
Finland	2
France	11
Germany	11
Ireland	1
Italy	3
Mexico	5
Norway	1
Poland	1
Portugal	2
Spain	5
Sweden	2
Switzerland	2
UK	7
USA	13
Venezuela	4

fg. 34 : Counting customers per country with a GROUP BY clause

Category Nam	NumberOfProduct
Beverages	12
Condiments	12
Confections	13
Dairy Products	10
Grains/Cereals	7
Meat/Poultry	6
Produce	5
Seafood	12

fg. 35 : Counting products by categories with alias columns

In this example **(Figure 35)** the GROUP BY clause actually gives instructions as to how to group the COUNT function, which in a previous example returned a single value. Obviously, we can use the GROUP BY clause with any other built-in function. For example, the following query will retrieve the average product price for each category of products:

```
SELECT Categories.CategoryName,
AVG (Products.UnitPrice) AS AveragePrice
FROM Categories INNER JOIN Products
ON Categories.CategoryID=Products.ProductID
GROUP BY Categories.CategoryName
```

Limiting Group Results with HAVING

It is possible to further limit the results of a grouped query. The HAVING clause enables us to specify conditions that will filter the group results that appear in the final record set.

By essentially eliminating records from the group, the HAVING clause resembles the behavior of the WHERE clause, which in turn limits the results of the SELECT statement. The HAVING clause is applied immediately after the GROUP BY statement and usually includes an aggregate function. This is especially useful when we filter data based on a summarized evaluation for each group. For example **(Figure 36)**, the following query creates a list of countries from which we have more than 5 customers:

```
SELECT Country
FROM Customers
GROUP BY Country
HAVING COUNT(CustomerID) >= 5
```

The HAVING clause applies on a per-group basis, filtering out those groups that don't match the condition. In comparison, the WHERE clause applies on a per-record basis, filtering out records. Therefore, while the WHERE clause restricts the record set with which the GROUP BY clause works, the HAVING clause affects only the display of the final results.

The HAVING condition can have more than one expression combined with any logical operators.

fg. 36 : Limiting group results with the HAVING clause

CHAPTER THREE
Entering and Modifying Data

Now that we have examined how to extract information from the database, the next step is to learn how to enter new data as well as modify existing information via SQL. Most RDBMSs provide tools that allow us to view database tables as well as add, modify and delete the data within those tables. While these tools are convenient when we work with small amounts of data, entering large amounts of data requires a different approach. Therefore, SQL offers three statements, INSERT INTO, UPDATE and DELETE, which will be the focus of this final section. As each statement name suggests, they are used for inserting, updating and deleting database data.

INSERT Information INTO the Database

The INSERT INTO statement provides us with an easy way to insert new data into an existing database. In the statement we first need to specify the table into which we want to insert data, followed by the columns into which data is to be inserted, and finally the actual data that needs to be inserted. The basic syntax for this statement is as follows:

```
INSERT INTO tableName (columnName1,
columnName2...)
VALUES (dataValue1, dataValue2,...)
```

The column names are separated by commas and placed in brackets after the table name. After this expression comes the VALUES statement and a comma-separated list of each data item that will be placed into the respective column. Character and date data must be placed in single quotes, while delimiters are not necessary for numerical values.

For example, the following statement adds an additional record to the Categories table, specifically the category "Vegetables."

```
INSERT INTO Categories (CategoryID,
CategoryName, Description)
VALUES (9, 'Vegetables', 'Seasoned vegetables')
```

We can specify the column names in any order we prefer. Regardless of column order, SQL will perform in the same way as long as the order of the column names set matches the data set. Conversely, the following SQL will also be valid:

```
INSERT INTO Categories (CategoryName,
CategoryID, Description)
VALUES ('Vegetables', 9, 'Seasoned vegetables')
```

If we insert the data in the same order as column names, it is also possible to completely leave out column names. The RDBMS will interpret the query just like its extended version.

```
INSERT INTO Categories
VALUES (9, 'Vegetables', 'Seasoned vegetables')
```

The advantage of not naming columns in the INSERT statement is that it saves typing and makes shorter SQL statements. The obvious disadvantage is the difficulty in seeing which data goes into which columns. After any of these statements, checking the Categories table with a properly structured SELECT statement will provide the following results **(Figure 37)**:

fg. 37

Category ID	Category Name	Description
1	Beverages	Soft drinks, coffees, teas, beers, and ales
2	Condiments	Sweet and savory sauces, relishes, spreads, and seasonings
3	Confections	Desserts, candies, and sweet breads
4	Dairy Products	Cheeses
5	Grains/Cereals	Breads, crackers, pasta, and cereal
6	Meat/Poultry	Prepared meats
7	Produce	Dried fruit and bean curd
8	Seafood	Seaweed and fish
9	Vegetables	Seasoned vegetables

Updating Data

Besides adding new records, we will eventually need to change the data in existing records. For this purpose we will use the UPDATE statement. Although similar, the main difference between inserting new data and updating existing data is the specification of the records that need to be changed. The records to be changed are defined with the WHERE clause, which will allow us to specify only those records that satisfy a certain condition. The SET clause will specify the exact columns in which data will be changed, separating multiple columns/value pairs with a comma. The generic syntax of the statement is as follows:

```
UPDATE tableName
SET columnName = value
WHERE condition
```

For example, let us say that one of our suppliers has changed the contact person responsible and has provided us with new data about the replacement. First, we need to identify the SupplierID, as this is the unique value that can be used in the WHERE clause to tell the database which specific records to update. However, it is not necessary to update every field in the record; it is sufficient to provide data only for the fields that are actually changing. The UPDATE statement allows us to define both the fields and the data that needs to be updated.

```
UPDATE Suppliers
SET
ContactName='Selene Pereira',
ContactTitle='Marketing Manager',
Phone='(172) 555 5345'
WHERE SupplierID=10
```

We need to consider that for situations in which the condition from the WHERE clause matches more than one record, all of the matching records will be changed in accordance with the instructions in the UPDATE statement.

Deleting Data from Tables

Deleting database data is easy. It is sufficient to first specify the table from which you will delete records, and then, if necessary, to add a WHERE clause to define the actual records to delete. Conversely, if we want to completely delete all records from a table, we can simply write the following SQL statement:

```
DELETE FROM Products;
```

If we execute the above statement, we will delete all the data from your Products table. To limit the deletion to only specific records, we can write the following query:

```
DELETE FROM Products
WHERE ProductID = 10
```

This SQL will delete all records from the Products table in which the ProductID has a value of 10. As this is a unique value, only one record will be deleted since there is only one product whose ProductID is ten. If we want to delete a range of records, we just need to modify the WHERE clause.

```
DELETE FROM Products
WHERE ProductID > =10 AND ProductID < 20
```

Nevertheless, deleting a record doesn't delete the references to that record in other tables. For example, although the Order Details table refers to products in the Products table, deleting a product from the Products table doesn't delete its respective reference in the Order Details table. This has to be executed with an additional SQL statement:

```
DELETE FROM [Order Details]
WHERE ProductID=10
```

If we are using ranges, then we modify the statement as follows:

```
DELETE FROM [Order Details]
WHERE ProductID > =10 AND ProductID < 20
```

CHAPTER FOUR
Defining Databases

The SQL language is not just limited to query and manipulation. It can also manipulate database objects starting from database creation. Many RDBMSs come with an easy-to-use interface that makes the task of creating new and manipulating existing database objects very simple and intuitive. With a few mouse clicks, and by entering a name, systems such as Access, SQL Server, Oracle, etc., allow us to create database objects without bothering with SQL syntax.

Creating/Deleting a Database

Before we can start working with a database, we need to actually create the database. There are plenty of options to achieve this goal, but we will focus only on the default, which in SQL is as easy as running the following statement:

```
CREATE DATABASE NorthWind
```

We use the CREATE DATABASE command followed by a database name, and we are all set. We have to mind how we name database objects, as different RDBMSs have different rules. The general guidelines for all systems are to use letters, numbers and the underscore character avoiding all other special characters, punctuation or spaces. Although they accept numbers, some systems don't allow the number to be the first character in the name, so we need to be mindful never to use names such as 1Customers. Finally, the names of all database objects have to be unique, as we cannot have two databases or two tables from the same database share a common name.

Deleting the database is as easy as creating the database. Nevertheless, we have to be mindful of the data that already exists in the database, as deleting the database will also delete all data it contains. Like the CREATE command, most RDBMSs have an easy-to-use user interface that allows us to drop a database using SQL. We use the DROP DATABASE command followed by the database name:

```
DROP DATABASE NorthWind
```

After creating a database the next step is adding tables. However, before we add any tables, we will look at the concept of data types.

Data Types

In the outside world we naturally categorize information into different types. When thinking of a price or the distance between two points, we think in terms of numbers. When looking up directions to a specific location, we expect textual information. The ***data type*** is determined based on its intended use. In databases, this classification helps the system to make more sense of its values. It is similar to what we naturally do in the real world, but in databases we categorize the data more formally.

Although we could treat all data as text and develop the database and future applications accordingly, the main reason for storing data with different data types is efficiency. Speed of access improves and storage space decreases when the database knows the type of data it has to process. For example, a large number such as 48903928 can be stored in 4 bytes of computer memory if it is treated as a numerical value, while storing the same number as character data will occupy twice as much space. Furthermore, the data type also tells the RDBMS what the user is expected to do with the data itself

Table 4 contains a small subset of the more commonly-used data types, which is more than enough to get us started. It briefly describes each data type followed by an example of how it is used in syntax form. The data categories themselves are explained in more detail in the following section.

> **NOTE**
>
> Defining data types across RDBMSs has slight variations. The approach presented in this book is in accordance with the SQL:2008 standard; for individual implementation please check the product documentation accordingly.

DATA TYPE	DESCRIPTION	EXAMPLE
CHARACTER	Stores data. A Character can be any letter, number, punctuation, special character, or empty space. We need to specify the number of characters that we intend to store in the field in advance.	Char (8)
VARYING CHARACTER	Stores text data similar to character, the only difference being the variable length of the text.	Varchar (12)
INTEGER	Stores a whole number between – 2 147 483 648 and 2 147 483 648	Int
DECIMAL	A floating point number allowing us to specify number length out of which we additionally define the number of decimal places.	Decimal (20,10)
DATE	Stores date. The date format is dependent on the regional settins.	Date
TIME	Stores the time in an Hour : Minutes : Seconds format	Time

Table. 4 : Fundamental data types

Characters

When we want to store text in a database field, we use one of the character data types. There are four possible variations, albeit we will only focus our explanation on two: fixed length and variable length. For example, if we use the code char(220), the RDBMS allocates enough memory to store 220 characters. If we store only 20 characters, the other 200 allocated places will be filled with empty spaces, which is rather wasteful. We might consider storing only 20 characters with char(20), but what happens when we need to store more, or maybe fewer? The alternative is the code varchar(220), as it will only use the actual amount of memory without pre-allocation.

Generally speaking, if the text data is expected to be of an approximate fixed length, then we will use the

NOTE

The char and varchar data types are limited to a maximum character storage of 255. For larger text we will need to use the memo (or text for MySQL) data type, which can store up to 65535 characters. We don't need to specify the actual number of characters this data type can hold. It is preset by the database system itself.

char data type as it allows for quick entry and manipulation. When the text data is of a variable length with a great scope, then we will use varchar.

Numerical Data

Integers, also known as whole numbers, are the easiest numbers to understand. In databases, the two most common integer data types are int and smallint. The difference between the two types is the size of the number they can store and the memory allocation needed to store the number. The smallint data type deals with a range between −32,768 and 32,767, whereas the int data type can handle a range between −2,147,483,648 and 2,147,483,647.

Floating numbers, also known as decimal numbers, can store the fractional parts of numbers. The two most common floating data types are real and decimal, for which, as with integers, the difference is number size and memory allocation. The real data type can store a range of numbers between −3.40E+38 and 3.40E+38 with a limit of 8 decimal places. This data type is very useful when we have huge numbers, but we are not too concerned about precision. When the number is too large to store precisely as a real data type, the database system converts it to the scientific notation with some loss of accuracy because of the dropped decimals. The decimal data type is similar to real, but it stores all the digits it can hold. Unlike with the real data type, storing a number that exceeds the capacity of the decimal data type will round of the number off instead of just dropping the digits. Due to this accuracy, knowing the flexibility of the decimal data type is important when we need to specify how many digits we want to store.

Date and Time

Time is a fairly easy data value to store. We need the hours, minutes and seconds, and we can store the time in the several formats such as HH:MM:SS, AM/PM, 24-hour, etc. On the other hand, dates have many possible variations, all of which depend on several inconsistent factors. For example, all of the following dates are valid: 8 Jun 2012, Jun 8, 2012, 12 June 2012, 12/06/2012, 06/12/2012, and 12-6-2012. In these examples the biggest problem arises when we specify the month by number instead of name. In America this data value would read as month/day, while in the EU this data value would be red as day/month. Therefore, it is advisable to avoid the date number format, and instead use the month's name or at least the abbreviation of its name.

In some cases RDBMSs don't keep date and time as separate values, but store them in one field. The date usually goes first, followed by the time in one of the

Defining Tables

Now that we have learned about creating databases and defining data types, we will finish this book by discussing how to create a new table, alter existing tables and delete tables that are no longer necessary.

To create a table we use the CREATE TABLE statement. In this statement we have to give the table a name and define each table column with a name and a data type. The basic syntax is as follows:

```
CREATE TABLE tableName
(
columnName1 datatype
columnName2 datatype
columnName3 datatype
...
)
```

> **NOTE**
>
> There are additional table options that can be managed in this statement, such as constraints, which are outside of the scope of this book.

First we write the CREATE TABLE statement, then the unique name of the table. In the next line we create a list defining each column in brackets. Each column definition is placed on its own line separated by a comma. If we were to create the Categories table, this would be the actual code:

```
CREATE TABLE Categories
(
CategoryID int,
CategoryName varchar (40),
Description varchar (255)
)
```

To change the properties of an existing table, we need the ALTER TABLE statement. With this statement we can modify table columns and, in some RDBMSs, even change the data type of an existing column. The basic syntax is shown below:

```
ALTER TABLE tableName
ADD columnName datatype
DROP COLUMN columnName
```

After the ALTER TABLE keyword, which essentially notifies the database system what is to happen, we provide the name of the table to be altered. Afterwards, when we want to add a new column, we continue the syntax with the ADD command and provide a column name with a data type, just like when we create a table. Deleting a column has a similar syntax, except we now tell the database which column to delete. The following example will add an ExpiryDate column to the Categories table:

```
ALTER TABLE Categories
ADD ExpiryDate date
```

As this column is unnecessary in the Categories table, we will delete it with the following statement:

```
ALTER TABLE Categories
DROP COLUMN ExpiryDate
```

We need to remember that dropping a column will permanently erase all data previously entered in that column.

> **NOTE**
>
> MS SQL Server uses datetime as data type, while Oracle stores both date and time into the date data type.

We follow this pattern when we use the DROP TABLE statement for deleting tables. The basic syntax is as follows

```
DROP TABLE tableName
```

To delete the Categories table we would simply write:

```
DROP TABLE Categories
```

However, dropping a table is not a light task to perform. Obviously, the data in the table will be deleted along with the table itself. What is not so obvious is that potential complications arise with related data in other tables.

CONCLUSION

This book covered a wide array of topics, but they all dealt with how to get information from a database. Initially, we were introduced to SQL, the language for communicating with a database. The focus was on using SQL as a query language, while the other aspects of the language were omitted.

We learned that the key to extracting data with SQL is the SELECT statement, which allows us to select the columns and tables from which to extract data. We now know how to filter with the WHERE clause by specifying any number of conditions in order to obtain the results that suit our particular needs. We were introduced to logical and comparison operators in order to better manage situational data conditions. We also learned how to manage the order of results in ascending or descending order, based on one or more columns with the ORDER BY clause.

By using the JOIN statements we tackled the slightly tricky topic of selecting data from more than one table. We managed to link two or more tables to form a new results set, and we learned the importance of the unknown (NULL) value.

We then summarized and aggregated data rather than getting results based on individual records. Central to this concept was the GROUP BY statement, which enables results to be based on groups of common data. In conjunction with SQL's aggregate functions such as COUNT, SUM, AVG, MAX, and MIN we learned how to manipulate data and calculate specific values. We also explored the HAVING clause, which filters out the result of groups using various conditions, much like a WHERE clause does for a SELECT statement. Conversely, we learned how to add new records to a database using the INSERT INTO statement, updated already existing data with the UPDATE statement, and learned about the DELETE statement, which allows us to delete all or specific records from a table.

Finally, we learned how to use SQL to define the structure of the database itself. We used the CREATE DATABASE statement to create a new database from scratch. We also learned about CREATE/ALTER/DROP TABLE commands to successfully manipulate the structures of tables.

GLOSSARY

Aggregate Function -
A function that produces a single result based on the contents of an entire set of table rows.

Alias -
A short substitute or nickname for a table/column name.

Column -
A table component that holds a single attribute of the table.

Comparison Operators -
Used to compare between values

Data Type -
A set of representable values.

Database -
A self-describing collection of records.

RDBMS -
A relational database management system.

Index -
A table of pointers used to locate rows rapidly in a data table.

Join -
A relational operator that combines data from multiple tables into a single result table.

Logical Operators -
Used to connect or change the truth-value of predicates to produce more complex predicates.

Metadata -
Data about the structure of the data in a database.

Predicate -
A statement that may be either logically true or logically false.

Query -
A question you ask about the data in a database.

Record -
A representation of some physical or conceptual object.

Row -
Another representation of a record.

SQL -
An industry standard data sublanguage, specifically designed to create, manipulate, and control relational databases.

Table -
A relation of data.

ABOUT CLYDEBANK TECHNOLOGY

ClydeBank Technology is a division of the multimedia-publishing firm ClydeBank Media LLC. ClydeBank Media's goal is to provide affordable, accessible information to a global market through different forms of media such as eBooks, paperback books and audio books. Company divisions are based on subject matter, each consisting of a dedicated team of researchers, writers, editors and designers.

The Technology division of ClydeBank Media is composed of contributors who are experts in their given disciplines. Contributors originate from diverse areas of the world to guarantee the presented information fosters a global perspective. Contributors have multiple years of experience in IT systems, networking, programming, web development and design, database development and management, graphic design and many other areas of discipline.

For more information, please visit us at
www.clydebankmedia.com
or email us at
contact info@clydebankmedia.com

MORE BOOKS BY CLYDEBANK TECHNOLOGY

WordPress Mastery
Exactly How To Become A WordPress Expert & Create Profitable Websites & Blogs In Minutes
URL : bit.ly/wordpress_mastery

Evernote Mastery
Exactly How To Use Evernote To Organize Your Life, Manage Your Day & Get Things Done
URL : bit.ly/evernote_mastery

Raspberry Pi For Beginners
Everything You Need To Know To Get The Most Out of Your Raspberry Pi
URL : bit.ly/rapberrypi

GET A FREE CLYDEBANK MEDIA AUDIOBOOK
+ 30 DAY FREE TRIAL TO AUDIBLE.COM

GET TITLES LIKE THIS ABSOLUTELY FREE:

- Business Plan Writing Guide
- ITIL for Beginners
- Stock Options for Beginners
- Scrum Quickstart Guide
- Project Management for Beginners
- 3D Printing Business

- LLC Quickstart Guide
- Lean Six Sigma Quickstart Guide
- Growing Marijuana for Beginners
- Social Security Simplified
- Medicare Simplified
- and more!

TO SIGN UP & GET YOUR FREE AUDIOBOOK, VISIT:
www.clydebankmedia.com/audible-trial

Made in the USA
Middletown, DE
23 December 2015